HAL•LEONARD

Jazz Play-Along®

Book and CD for B♭, E♭, C and Bass Clef Instruments

JOHN LENNON

T0085338

VOLUME 189

BOOK

Arranged and Produced by Mark Taylor

Cover photo by David Gahr/Getty Images

ISBN 978-1-4950-0381-3

HAL•LEONARD®
CORPORATION

7777 W. BLUEMOUND RD. P.O. BOX 13819 MILWAUKEE, WI 53213

In Australia Contact:
Hal Leonard Australia Pty. Ltd.
4 Lentara Court
Cheltenham, Victoria, 3192 Australia
Email: ausadmin@halleonard.com.au

Visit Hal Leonard Online at
www.halleonard.com

JOHN LENNON

Volume 189

Arranged and Produced
by Mark Taylor

Featured Players:

Graham Breedlove–Trumpet
John Desalme–Saxes
Tony Nalker–Piano
Jim Roberts–Guitar
Paul Henry–Bass
Todd Harrison–Drums

Recorded at Bias Studios, Springfield, Virginia
Bob Dawson, Engineer

HOW TO USE THE CD:

Each song has <u>two</u> tracks:

1) Split Track/Melody

Woodwind, Brass, Keyboard, and **Mallet Players** can use this track as a learning tool for melody style and inflection.

Bass Players can learn and perform with this track – remove the recorded bass track by turning down the volume on the LEFT channel.

Keyboard and **Guitar Players** can learn and perform with this track – remove the recorded piano part by turning down the volume on the RIGHT channel.

2) Full Stereo Track

Soloists or **Groups** can learn and perform with this accompaniment track with the RHYTHM SECTION only.

CD

1 : SPLIT TRACK/MELODY
2 : FULL STEREO TRACK

A DAY IN THE LIFE

WORDS AND MUSIC BY JOHN LENNON
AND PAUL McCARTNEY

C VERSION

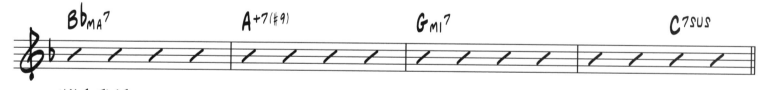

IMAGINE

WORDS AND MUSIC BY
JOHN LENNON

CD
3 : SPLIT TRACK/MELODY
4 : FULL STEREO TRACK

C VERSION

MEDIUM ROCK BALLAD

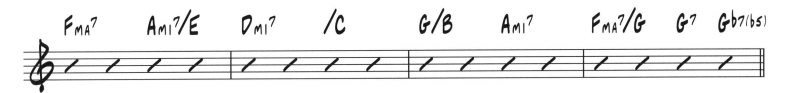

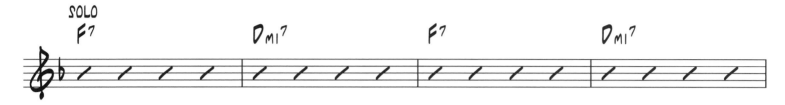

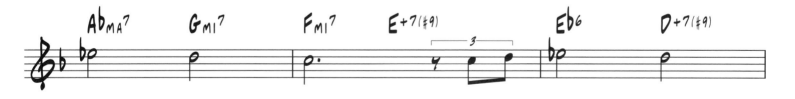

LUCY IN THE SKY WITH DIAMONDS

CD
◆ 9 : SPLIT TRACK/MELODY
◆ 10 : FULL STEREO TRACK

WORDS AND MUSIC BY JOHN LENNON
AND PAUL McCARTNEY

C VERSION

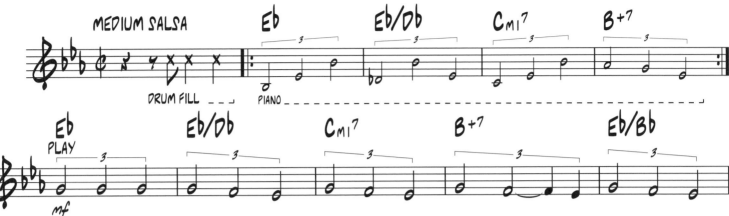

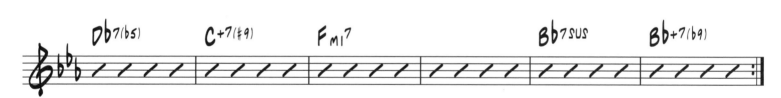

CD

11 : SPLIT TRACK/MELODY
12 : FULL STEREO TRACK

C VERSION

(JUST LIKE)
STARTING OVER

WORDS AND MUSIC BY
JOHN LENNON

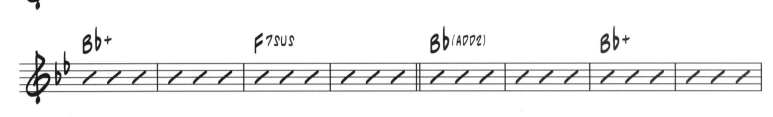

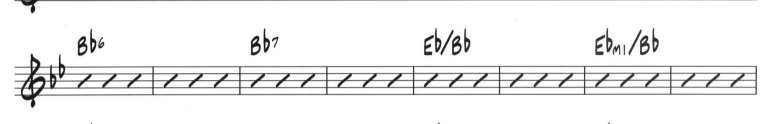

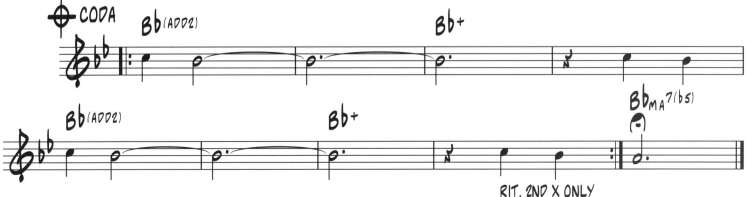

STRAWBERRY FIELDS FOREVER

WORDS AND MUSIC BY JOHN LENNON
AND PAUL McCARTNEY

CD
13: SPLIT TRACK/MELODY
14: FULL STEREO TRACK

C VERSION

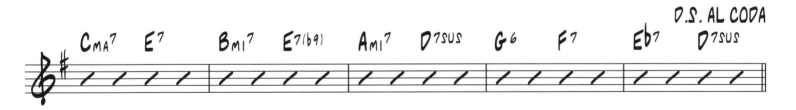

CD

15 : SPLIT TRACK/MELODY
16 : FULL STEREO TRACK

WATCHING THE WHEELS

WORDS AND MUSIC BY
JOHN LENNON

C VERSION

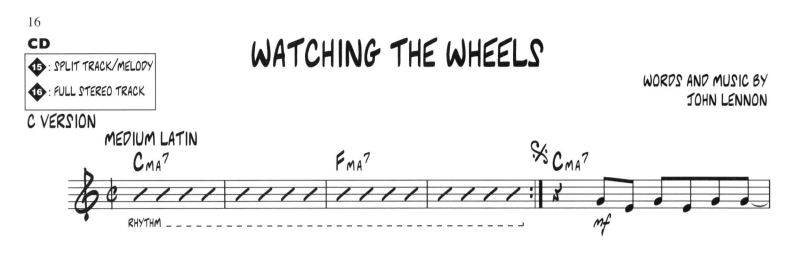

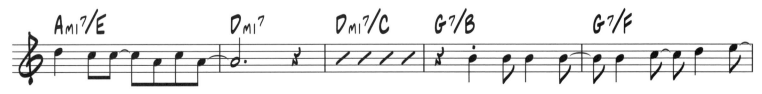

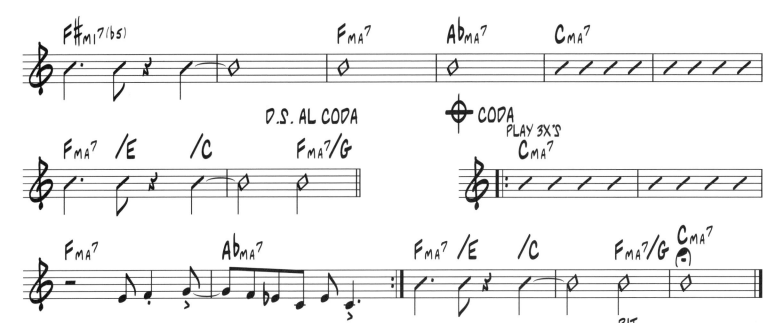

WOMAN

CD

◆17: SPLIT TRACK/MELODY
◆18: FULL STEREO TRACK

WORDS AND MUSIC BY
JOHN LENNON

C VERSION

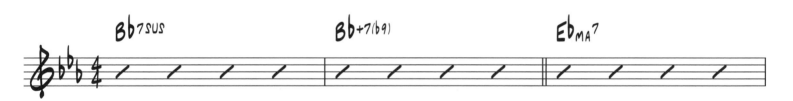

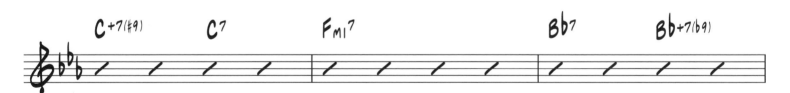

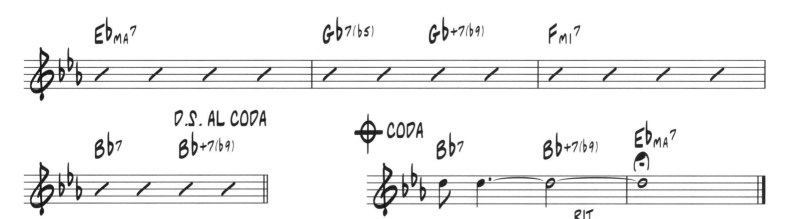

YOU'VE GOT TO HIDE YOUR LOVE AWAY

WORDS AND MUSIC BY JOHN LENNON
AND PAUL McCARTNEY

CD
19 : SPLIT TRACK/MELODY
20 : FULL STEREO TRACK

C VERSION

21

Jealous Guy

WORDS AND MUSIC BY
JOHN LENNON

Jealous Guy

WORDS AND MUSIC BY
JOHN LENNON

A Day in the Life

WORDS AND MUSIC BY JOHN LENNON
AND PAUL McCARTNEY

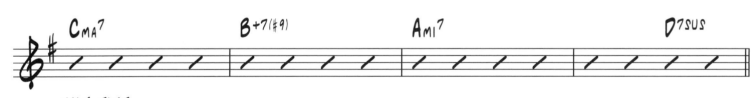

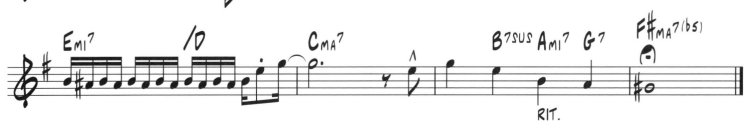

IMAGINE

WORDS AND MUSIC BY
JOHN LENNON

CD
- ◆3 : SPLIT TRACK/MELODY
- ◆4 : FULL STEREO TRACK

Bb VERSION

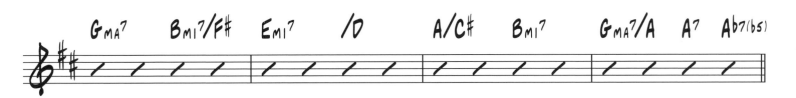

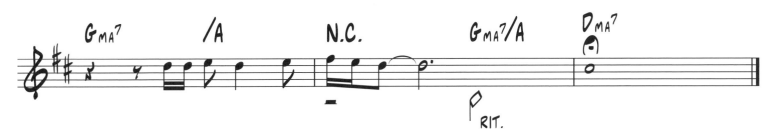

INSTANT KARMA

WORDS AND MUSIC BY
JOHN LENNON

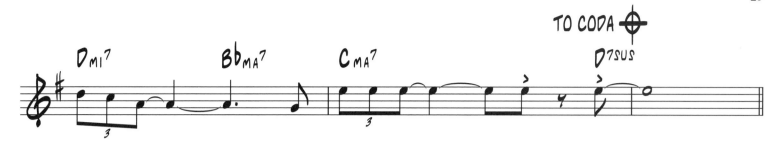

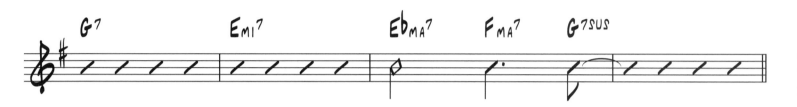

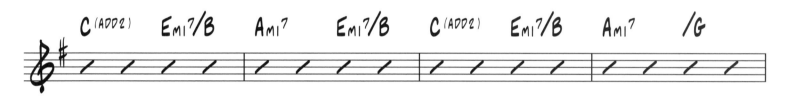

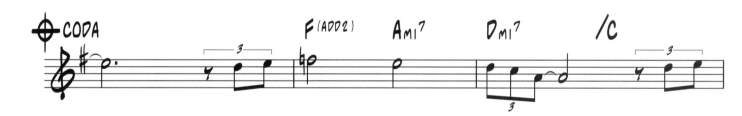

LUCY IN THE SKY WITH DIAMONDS

WORDS AND MUSIC BY JOHN LENNON
AND PAUL McCARTNEY

CD
- ◆ 9 : SPLIT TRACK/MELODY
- ◆ 10 : FULL STEREO TRACK

Bb VERSION

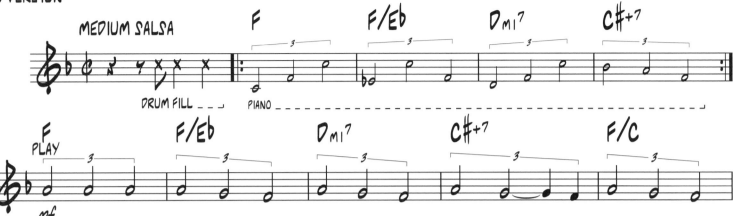

CD
- 🎵 11 : SPLIT TRACK/MELODY
- 🎵 12 : FULL STEREO TRACK

Bb VERSION

(JUST LIKE)
STARTING OVER

WORDS AND MUSIC BY
JOHN LENNON

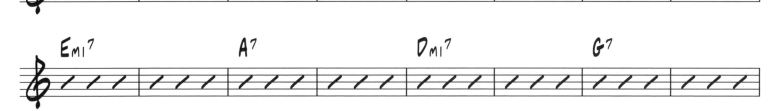
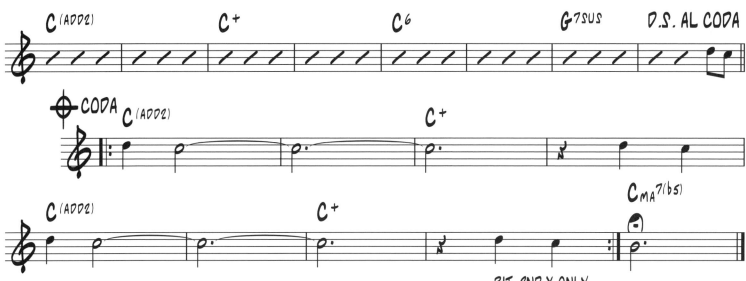

RIT. 2ND X ONLY

STRAWBERRY FIELDS FOREVER

CD
13 : SPLIT TRACK/MELODY
14 : FULL STEREO TRACK

Bb VERSION

WORDS AND MUSIC BY JOHN LENNON
AND PAUL McCARTNEY

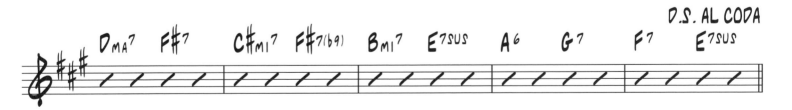

WATCHING THE WHEELS

WORDS AND MUSIC BY
JOHN LENNON

Bb VERSION

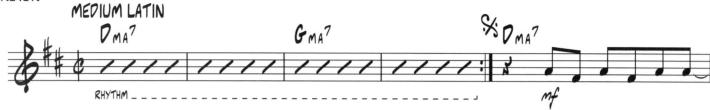

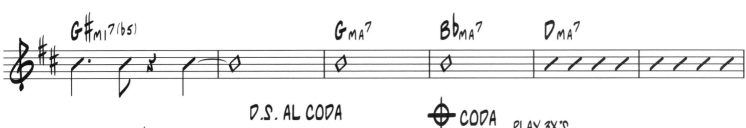

WOMAN

WORDS AND MUSIC BY
JOHN LENNON

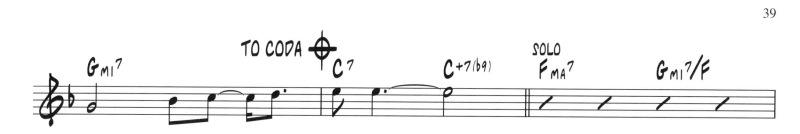

You've Got to Hide Your Love Away

CD
19 : SPLIT TRACK/MELODY
20 : FULL STEREO TRACK

Bb VERSION

WORDS AND MUSIC BY JOHN LENNON
AND PAUL McCARTNEY

MEDIUM LATIN JAZZ WALTZ

C#6(b5)   Eb6   SOLO   C6   G6/B   Bb6   Am i7

Dm i7   G7sus   C6   G6/B

Bb6   Am i7   Dm i7   C6/E   Fma7   G7sus

C6   G6/B   Bb6   Am i7   /G   Fma7   E7(#9)

Eb6   Dm i7   G7sus   F#m i7(b5)   F7(b5)   Bb7   Am i7

Abma7   C#ma7   Dm i7   G7   Fma7

Em i7   Dm i7   C6   Fma7   Eb7(b5)

Dm i7   C#7(b5)   C6   E+7(#9)

F6   A+7(#9)   Abma7   G7sus   D.S. AL CODA

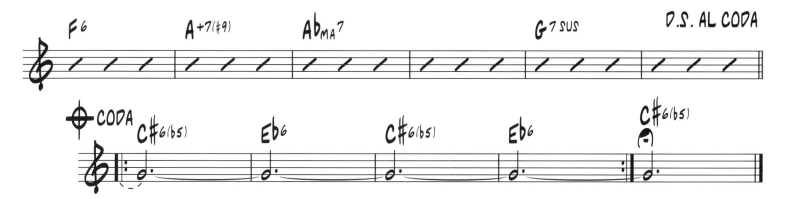

CODA   C#6(b5)   Eb6   C#6(b5)   Eb6   C#6(b5)

42

A Day in the Life

RIT.

IMAGINE

WORDS AND MUSIC BY
JOHN LENNON

Eb VERSION

MEDIUM ROCK BALLAD

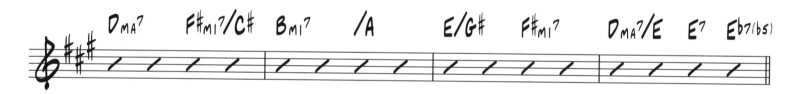

INSTANT KARMA

WORDS AND MUSIC BY
JOHN LENNON

Eb VERSION

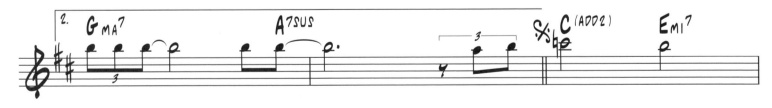

CD

9 : SPLIT TRACK/MELODY
10 : FULL STEREO TRACK

LUCY IN THE SKY WITH DIAMONDS

WORDS AND MUSIC BY JOHN LENNON
AND PAUL McCARTNEY

Eb VERSION

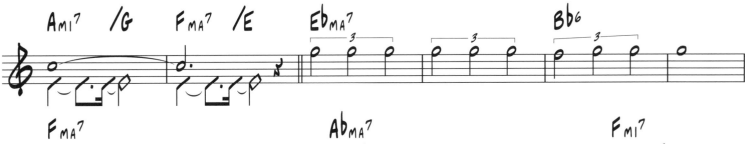

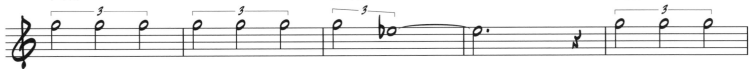

(JUST LIKE) STARTING OVER

WORDS AND MUSIC BY
JOHN LENNON

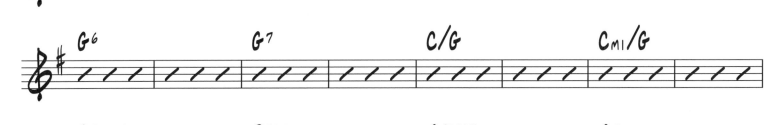

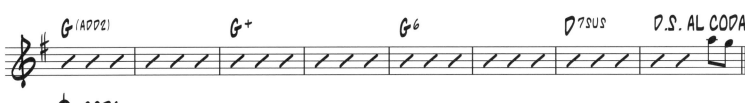

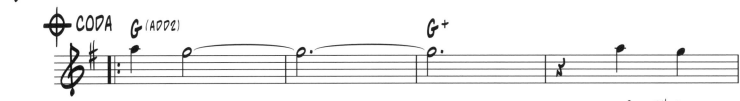

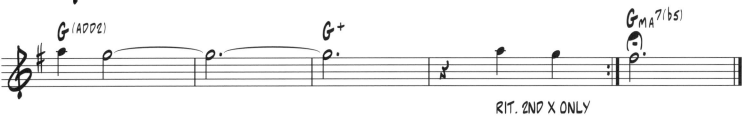

RIT. 2ND X ONLY

STRAWBERRY FIELDS FOREVER

WORDS AND MUSIC BY JOHN LENNON
AND PAUL McCARTNEY

CD
13 : SPLIT TRACK/MELODY
14 : FULL STEREO TRACK

Eb VERSION

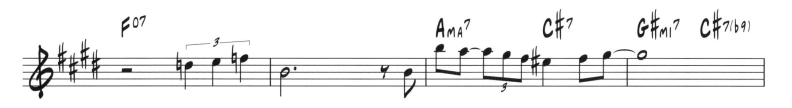

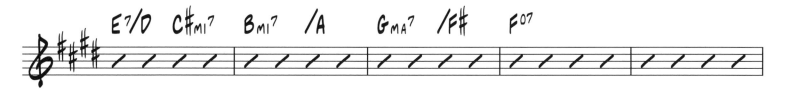

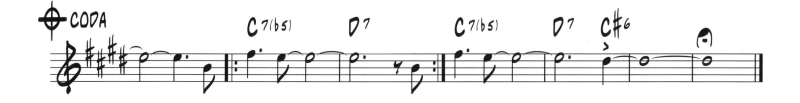

Watching the Wheels

WORDS AND MUSIC BY
JOHN LENNON

CD

- **15** : SPLIT TRACK/MELODY
- **16** : FULL STEREO TRACK

Eb VERSION

WOMAN

WORDS AND MUSIC BY
JOHN LENNON

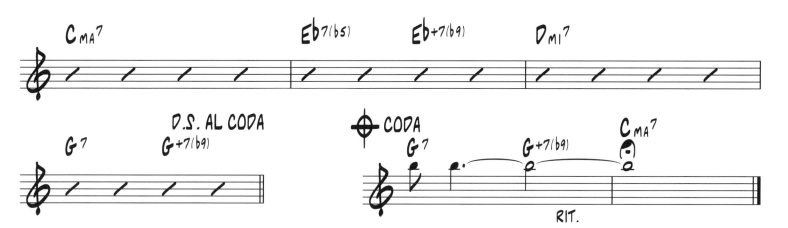

CD

19 : SPLIT TRACK/MELODY
20 : FULL STEREO TRACK

YOU'VE GOT TO HIDE YOUR LOVE AWAY

WORDS AND MUSIC BY JOHN LENNON
AND PAUL McCARTNEY

Eb VERSION

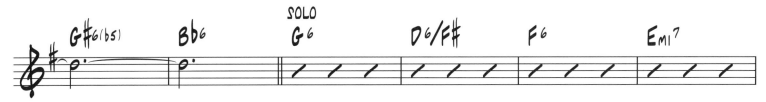
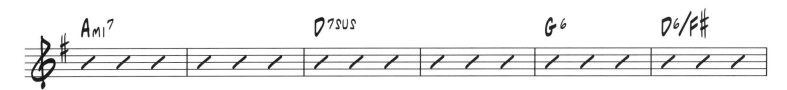

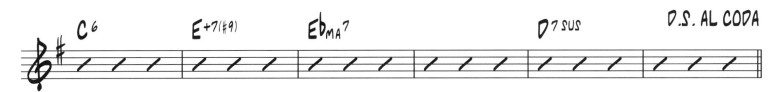

Jealous Guy

Jealous Guy

A Day in the Life

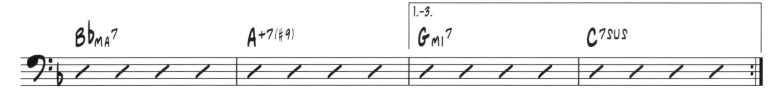

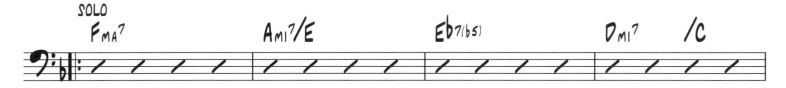

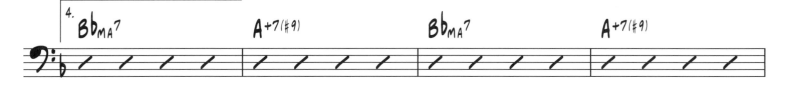

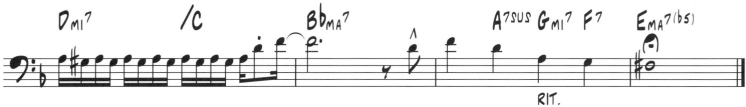

IMAGINE

WORDS AND MUSIC BY
JOHN LENNON

INSTANT KARMA

WORDS AND MUSIC BY
JOHN LENNON

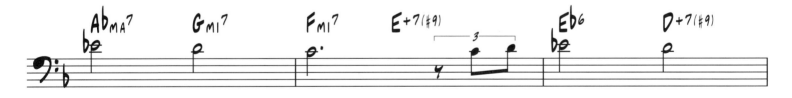

LUCY IN THE SKY WITH DIAMONDS

CD
🔷 9 : SPLIT TRACK/MELODY
🔷 10 : FULL STEREO TRACK

WORDS AND MUSIC BY JOHN LENNON
AND PAUL McCARTNEY

𝄢: C VERSION

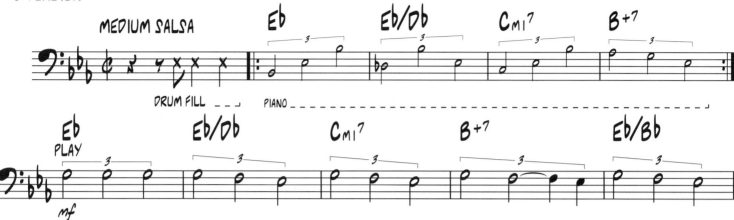

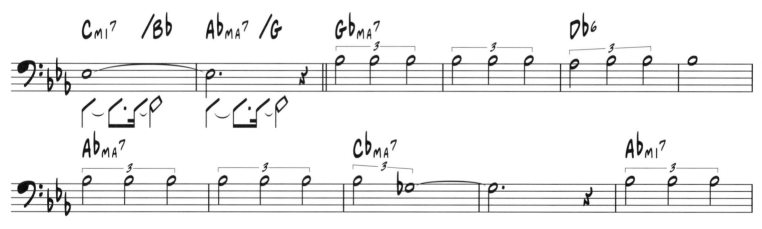

CD

(JUST LIKE)
STARTING OVER

WORDS AND MUSIC BY
JOHN LENNON

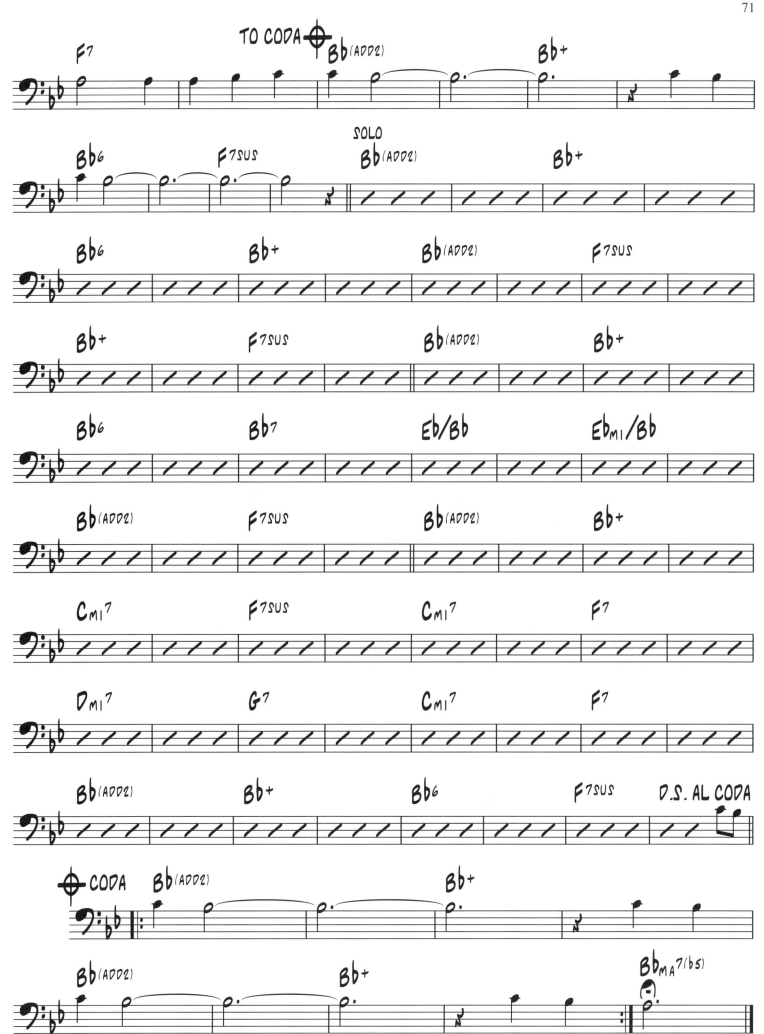

RIT. 2ND X ONLY

CD

13 : SPLIT TRACK/MELODY
14 : FULL STEREO TRACK

STRAWBERRY FIELDS FOREVER

WORDS AND MUSIC BY JOHN LENNON
AND PAUL McCARTNEY

𝄢: C VERSION

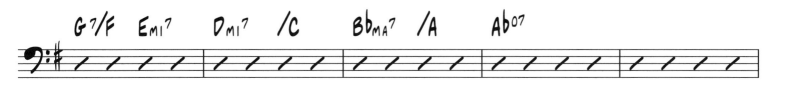

CD

WATCHING THE WHEELS

WORDS AND MUSIC BY
JOHN LENNON

𝄢: C VERSION

MEDIUM LATIN

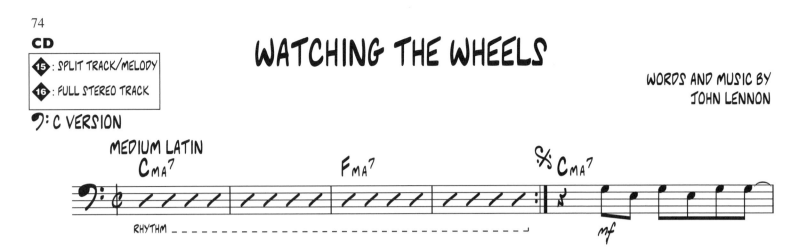

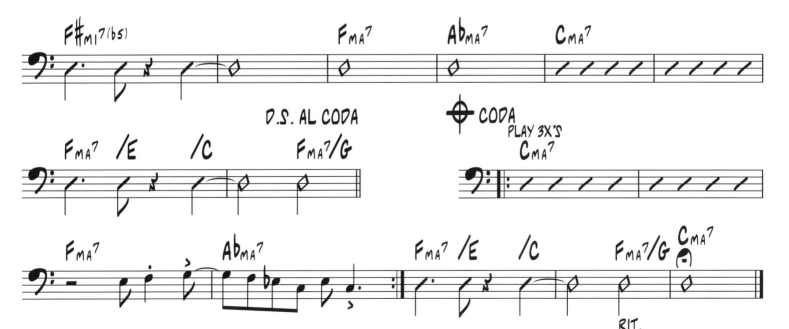

WOMAN

WORDS AND MUSIC BY
JOHN LENNON

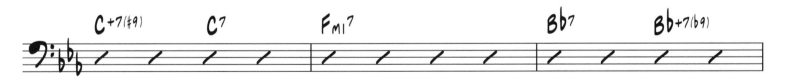

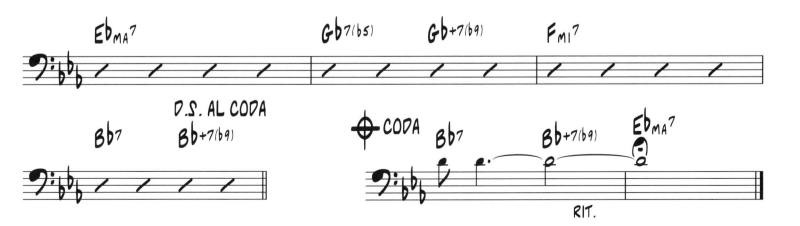

You've Got to Hide Your Love Away

CD
19 : SPLIT TRACK/MELODY
20 : FULL STEREO TRACK

WORDS AND MUSIC BY JOHN LENNON
AND PAUL McCARTNEY

𝄢 : C VERSION

SOLO

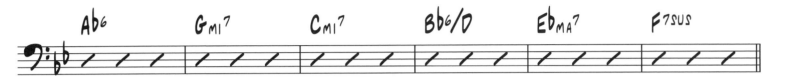

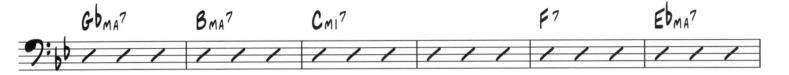

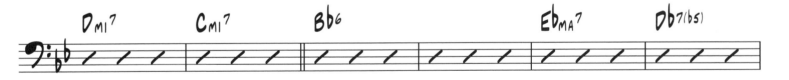

D.S. AL CODA